THE
COMMONWEALTH
OF INDEPENDENT STATES

Mary Jane Behrends Clark

THE MILLBROOK PRESS
Brookfield, Connecticut

Published by The Millbrook Press
2 Old New Milford Road
Brookfield, CT 06804
© 1992 Blackbirch Graphics, Inc.

5 4 3

Created and produced in association with Blackbirch Graphics.
Series Editor: Bruce S. Glassman

Library of Congress Cataloging-in-Publication Data
Clark, Mary Jane Behrends.
    The Commonwealth of Independent States / by Mary Jane Behrends Clark.
        p.   cm. — (Headliners)
    Includes bibliographical references and index.
    Summary: Provides background on eleven countries that were formerly part of the Soviet Union and examines the problems they face since declaring independence in 1991.
    ISBN 1-56294-081-3   (lib. bdg.)
    1. Commonwealth of Independent States—Juvenile literature. 2. Former Soviet republics—Juvenile literature. [1. Commonwealth of Independent States. 2. Former Soviet republics.] I. Title. II. Series.
DK1.5.C57   1992
947.085'4—dc20   92-20745
                                                                         CIP
                                                                         AC

Contents

Chapter 7

New Nations Join the World

The breakup of the Soviet Union at the end of 1991 suddenly placed fifteen newly independent republics on the world scene. In place of the world's most powerful Communist state, there were now fifteen countries with individual political, economic, and cultural agendas—and all were going through complex growing pains as they began independent statehood.

As parts of the Soviet Union, they had been linked together economically and in many other ways. Now, with old ties broken, they faced economic hardship and ethnic rivalries that sometimes erupted into violence. Under Communist rule, they had learned to be suspicious of the West. Now they turned to the West for help and began to adopt ideas—democracy, economic reform—that had been forbidden by the old Soviet government.

The new republics faced an uncertain future. Recognizing how deeply they had depended on each other in the past, eleven of the fifteen banded together in December 1991 to form the Commonwealth of Independent States. The new commonwealth was neither a country nor a government. Instead, it was a unique coalition of diverse peoples and governments who came together for specific purposes. Whether the commonwealth could achieve its goals—or, in fact, survive—remained unclear.

In 1991, fifteen newly independent republics began a very different way of life.

Opposite:
A Ukrainian man steps on the flag of the Soviet Union at a demonstration in Kiev.

The Soviet Collapse

A majority of the fifteen republics had declared their independence days after conservative Communist party members attempted to overthrow Soviet President Mikhail Gorbachev in August 1991. Gorbachev had attempted to reform the inefficient Soviet system, introducing democratic measures and lessening the government's grip on the economy. Fearing that these reforms would put them out of power, a group of Communist hardliners placed him under house arrest and announced that they were in control of the country. But Soviet citizens took their nation's future into their own hands. They flooded into the streets in defiance of martial law and formed barricades to protect Russian president Boris Yeltsin and other elected leaders. After three tense days, the coup leaders gave up.

With the coup ended, Gorbachev was restored to power—but only temporarily. In the days that followed, opposition to the Communist party spread like wildfire.

Soviet tanks sealed off part of Moscow during the coup of August 1991.

By the final week in August, the party had lost control of the government, and all party activities were suspended. Meanwhile, movements by the republics to separate from the Soviet Union gained strength. One by one, most of the republics declared their independence, and the seventy-year-old Soviet Union ceased to exist.

The Commonwealth Is Born

The birth of the commonwealth came in the winter after the August coup.

On December 8, 1991, the various leaders of Russia, Byelorussia (later to become Belarus), and Ukraine met in a forest retreat near the Byelorussian city of Brest and declared the end of the Union of Soviet Socialist Republics. There the three Slavic leaders, Boris Yeltsin of Russia, Stanislav Shushkevich of Byelorussia, and Leonid Kravchuk of Ukraine, argued that their republics had the authority to take the step to dismantle the Soviet state because they had been its founding members. The collective size of the three republics, which together accounted for eighty percent of the Soviet Union's area and seventy-three percent of its population, also gave their decision weight.

The three presidents signed an accord that would help them in their "striving to found democratic legal states." Among their agreements were the following:

- All members of the commonwealth would function as independent states and respect each other's territories and borders. Each member would retain its sovereignty, right to self-determination, and right to noninterference in its internal affairs.
- Each member would guarantee its citizens equal rights and freedom regardless of nationality and other differences.
- Member states would respect the rights of ethnic minorities within their boundaries and offer them protection.

Russian President Boris Yeltsin shakes hands with Belarus leader Stanislav Shushkevich at their meeting in Brest. At that meeting, Russia, Ukraine, and Belarus signed the "death certificate" of the Soviet Union.

- All members would work toward achieving complete nuclear disarmament and cooperate to encourage international peace.
- All states of the former USSR could join the commonwealth, as could any other state that shares its goals and principles. Any state could also leave the commonwealth on a year's notice.
- Member states would create central coordinating groups to determine and conduct the commonwealth's foreign and immigration policies, a common economic community, communication and transport systems, environmental protection plans, and law enforcement.
- The commonwealth would honor all international agreements and treaties of the former USSR.
- Any state that signed the commonwealth agreement would abolish all laws of the USSR from its territories.
- The commonwealth would base its central committee in the Byelorussian city of Brest (away from Moscow).

Any hope Soviet President Gorbachev had of creating a political union on his own terms was destroyed with the signing of the commonwealth agreement. The day after the agreement was announced, Gorbachev held a televised news conference. "It is illegitimate and dangerous to declare that the [Soviet Union's] legal norms are no longer valid, " he said. "It can only intensify the chaos and anarchy in society."

But Gorbachev soon faced the inevitable. On December 17, 1991, the Soviet president and the Russian republic president held a two-hour private discussion. After the talk, Yeltsin announced that Gorbachev knew the end of the Soviet Union was at hand. The two agreed that the Soviet Union would cease to exist by 1992.

The effective end of the Soviet Union actually came on December 21, when eleven Soviet republics signed agreements to create the commonwealth. The eleven active republics were Russia, Ukraine, Belarus, Kazakhstan, Uzbekistan, Turkmenistan, Tajikistan, Kyrgyzstan, Moldova, Azerbaijan, and Armenia. (The republic of Georgia was embroiled in a civil war and did not sign. The Baltic republics of Latvia, Estonia, and Lithuania also preferred to remain independent.)

The pact was signed at a meeting of the republics' presidents in Alma-Ata, the capital of the Central Asian republic of Kazakhstan. At Alma-Ata, the presidents

On December 21, 1991, eleven former Soviet republics signed an agreement in Alma-Ata to create the Commonwealth of Independent States.

reached a consensus on several critical points. Among other things, they agreed to the following principles:

- The commonwealth was not in itself a state. It was an alliance of fully independent bodies. Policy was to be set by a committee of representatives.
- The individual states would own the former Soviet government's non-military facilities on their soil.
- Ukraine and Belarus would keep the separate memberships they had held in the United Nations since 1945. Russia would take over the Soviet membership and its seat on the Security Council. The other eight commonwealth states would seek membership in the United Nations.
- The commonwealth would honor the USSR's arms-control commitments.

On December 23, Gorbachev met again with Yeltsin in the Kremlin, this time to discuss the final transfer of power. Questions to be worked out included the distribution of Soviet state property, archives and assets, and strategic and conventional military forces. When they were done, Gorbachev turned over to the Russian president the Soviet nuclear war codes.

In his resignation speech, Gorbachev evaluated the historic changes that had occurred during his six years in power. In closing, he said, "We are the heirs of a great civilization, and its rebirth into a new, modern, and dignified life now depends on one and all. . . . Some mistakes could surely have been avoided. Many things could have been done better. But I am convinced that sooner or later our common efforts will bear fruit. Our nations will live in a prosperous and democratic society."

The Soviet Union, formed in 1922, was officially dissolved with little ceremony shortly after Gorbachev's resignation. On New Year's Eve, 1991, the giant red Soviet flag emblazoned with a hammer and sickle was replaced by the red, white, and blue flag of pre-revolutionary Russia—perhaps forever.

Gorbachev After the Coup

Mikhail Gorbachev resigned his leadership on December 25, 1991.

"I have firmly stood for independence, self-rule of nations, for the sovereignty of the republics, but at the same time for preservation of the union state, the unity of the country," Mikhail Gorbachev explained in his televised resignation speech on Christmas Day, 1991. But, as he added, "events went a different way." The Commonwealth of Independent States was established only days earlier, dissolving the Soviet Union and his post as its president.

Russian president Yeltsin announced that Gorbachev would have no official function in the new commonwealth, which meant that the Soviet president was not only resigning his post but also retiring from public office altogether.

Gorbachev and his wife Raisa moved into a three-room Moscow apartment in January 1991. They continued to enjoy some state privileges, such as a country house, bodyguards, and a limousine. But Gorbachev would have to supplement his monthly pension of 3,900 rubles, a once generous sum that was worth only about $40 at the 1992 exchange rates, by going to work as a private citizen.

At the age of sixty-one, Gorbachev took a job as president of an international policy institute. He also began writing a monthly column for the internationally distributed Italian newspaper *La Stampa*. Still popular and respected around the world, he planned several lecture tours, including one to the United States. A British film company bought the rights to a movie about Gorbachev's life. The former Soviet leader negotiated with publishers to sell his book about the final days of the Soviet Union. These activities were expected to bring Gorbachev several million dollars.

Out of power, Gorbachev said that he found comfort in long country walks, friends, concerts, books (some 20,000 books and documents filled his apartment), and Raisa. "Raisa Maximova and I have more time together," he told a *Time* magazine reporter two months after leaving office. "The rest doesn't matter . . . . over all these years, we have stayed like friends." Mrs. Gorbachev, on the other hand, claimed that they did not have enough time together because her husband was always working.

The focus of Gorbachev's work, even out of public office, has been the future of his country. Whether he will again have an official role in shaping that future is unknown. In a May 1992 visit to Japan, Gorbachev openly spoke about a possible comeback. But his friends and advisors have said that he expected only to be an outspoken elder statesman.

So far Gorbachev has spoken out in criticism of President Bush for saying that the United States had "won" the Cold War. "My reply to this would be that the long years we spent plunged in the Cold War made losers of us all, " Gorbachev wrote in his first column for *La Stampa*. "And in our own time, the world's rejection of confrontation and hostility has made us all winners."

In May 1992, Gorbachev made a historic speech at Westminster College in Fulton, Missouri. Forty-six years before, at the same college, Winston Churchill had delivered his famous "iron curtain" speech formally declaring the beginning of the Cold War. Gorbachev's address marked its end. The end of the Cold War, he proclaimed, "was altogether a victory for common sense, reason, democracy, and common human values."

Chapter 2

From Czars to Freedom

The collapse of the Soviet Union marked the end of an ancient empire. A thousand years ago, Russia was a small region in Europe. As it grew gradually by adding territory on all sides, many different peoples fell under its rule. Through the centuries, these non-Russian cultures tried to keep their customs and languages intact, never losing their fierce devotion to their own cultural identities.

For hundreds of years, Russia was ruled by emperors, called czars, who had complete control over Russian life. Under the czars' rule, the country was mostly cut off from the industrial progress made in Western Europe in the 1800s. Its population was made up mostly of poor and uneducated peasants who lived harsh lives, farming the land with the same hand tools their ancestors had used. These hard-working people expressed their feelings in sad, beautiful songs, in colorful festivals, and in lively folk dances that helped them forget the hardships they endured under harsh rule.

Industrial progress may have been slow under the czars' rule, but the arts flourished. Many great works of literature and music were produced by such artists as Anton Chekhov, Fyodor Dostoevsky, Peter Ilyich Tchaikovsky, and Modest Moussorgsky, to name but a few.

The Soviet Union had a rich history of struggle, domination, and oppression.

Opposite:
Ukrainian workers take down a giant statue of Vladimir Lenin, one of the founders of Soviet communism. The statue was over forty feet high and weighed more than three hundred tons.

Revolution

In 1917, revolutionary forces drove Czar Nicholas II and his family from power. The Bolsheviks (later called Communists), led by Vladimir Lenin, seized the government. The new government took control of the farms, factories, and all other means of production. The Bolsheviks turned Russia into the first Communist country.

From 1918 to 1920, a violent civil war between Communists and anti-Communists tore Russia apart. Several outlying regions attempted to break away from the new government. The Baltic states of Estonia, Latvia, and Lithuania did gain their independence from Russian rule, but only until 1940. Eventually, the Communists won control of the Russian Empire and established the Soviet Union. Their government, a "dictatorship of workers and peasants," was actually run by top Communist officials.

For most of its history, the Soviet Union was made up of fifteen republics. These republics were Armenia, Azerbaijan, Byelorussia, Estonia, Georgia, Kazakhstan, Kirghizia, Latvia, Lithuania, Moldavia, Russia, Tadzhikistan, Turkmenistan, Ukraine, and Uzbekistan. Each union

Communist leaders Vladimir Lenin (left) and Joseph Stalin sit together in Gorky Park, Russia, in 1922.

republic had its own government, but the real power rested with the Soviet central government in Moscow. The central government, as well as other levels of government, was strictly controlled by the Communist party.

Joseph Stalin, who headed the USSR from 1924 to 1953, created a government that relied on cruelty and fear to rule its people. Soviet citizens were forced by many means to adhere to strict Communist principles. Perhaps the most infamous of these means were the series of "purges" that Stalin ordered throughout his years of leadership. To "purge," or remove, any lingering opposition to communism, state police would round up, imprison, torture, and even kill citizens. The most devastating of these raids, now called the "Great Purge," began in 1934.

Later Soviet rulers were less harsh than Stalin, but repression remained a fact of Soviet life. And although the government launched massive programs to build up industries, Communist rule caused severe economic problems, particularly in providing consumer goods. Relying on government ownership and central planning, the Soviet Union faced frequent shortages of basic goods and its standard of living lagged well behind that of Western nations.

The Rise of Nationalism

When looking at the former Soviet Union, the most important thing to understand is that a Soviet "nation" existed primarily in Communist propaganda. In reality, a Communist ruling elite dominated by Russian nationals dictated to all the diverse nations of the union. Still, try as they did to "Russify" these nations, the Communists were not able to wipe out strong ethnic identities.

By the 1980s, gargantuan economic problems riddled the Soviet Union. Many people saw that communism as an economic system did not work. It was also apparent that a system in which people could not freely express their ideas and beliefs could not flourish. When years of

The Baltic Republics

During the Communist "thaw" of 1990, the Baltic republics of Estonia, Latvia, and Lithuania began more intense efforts to secede from the Soviet Union. Viewing themselves as part of Europe and of European culture, the Baltic countries were more attuned to the democratic politics of the West than the authoritarian traditions of Russia. And they resented Soviet control.

The Baltics, annexed by the Russian Empire in 1721, had been granted independence by the Soviet government in 1918. However, a pact in 1940 between Stalin and German Nazi leader Adolf Hitler carved up Eastern Europe and handed the Baltic republics to the USSR. The Baltic people considered this an act of piracy. The United States and much of the world community refused to recognize the incorporation of the Baltic states into the Soviet Union.

Many Estonians, Latvians, and Lithuanians—victims of the terrorism of Stalin and Hitler—fled to Sweden and other countries. Others were harshly treated during the Soviet collectivization drive in the 1950s. Hundreds of thousands were forced into labor camps. Collectivization was a Soviet program whereby privately owned farms were seized for collective ownership by the peasants who worked on them.

After decades of repression, tension and resentment grew. In 1989 there were signals of "independence fever." The most dramatic example was a massive demonstration on August 23, the fiftieth anniversary of the Hitler-Stalin pact. More than one million people formed a human chain 370 miles (595 kilometers) long, a freedom chain linking the three Baltic capitals. People joined hands and passed on the word *freedom* until it traveled from one person to the next from Tallinn (Estonia) in the north, through Riga (Latvia) in the middle, to Vilnius (Lithuania) in the south. That one million people took part in the chain meant that one out of every five Latvians, Lithuanians, and Estonians took part—virtually someone from every family.

Lithuania took the plunge first. On March 11, 1990, it declared independence. The Lithuanian parliament broke into applause at its own defiance of Moscow, Gorbachev, and the Soviet system.

Retaliation from Moscow came in the form of Soviet tanks rumbling through the streets of Vilnius, a cut-off of Soviet gas and oil supplies, and an economic embargo. Eventually, Gorbachev realized he could not extinguish the burning desire for freedom. In declaring independence, the Lithuanians felt they were righting a historical wrong. Latvia and Estonia soon followed Lithuania in declaring independence.

The Baltic republics of Estonia, Latvia, and Lithuania did not join the Commonwealth of Independent States when it was first created in 1991. Most of the Baltic citizens had struggled so long for independence that joining yet another union held little appeal. Although they are considered to have the highest standard of living of any of the former Soviet republics, the Baltic states have struggled a great deal to recover from the effects of fifty years of Soviet control.

stagnation and mismanagement made change a necessity, Mikhail Gorbachev tried to save the Soviet system by making it more humane and efficient. Taking control in 1985, Gorbachev instituted his policies of *glasnost*, a new openness, and *perestroika*, his plan for restructuring. While these policies brought some needed reforms, they also allowed nationalism and ethnic rivalries, suppressed for years, to re-emerge. They led to violent clashes in Azerbaijan and other republics.

There were other problems as well. Gorbachev succeeded in introducing a measure of democracy to Soviet life. The central government was restructured to lessen the grip of the Communist party, and open elections were held for some posts. But Gorbachev was unwilling to do away with the old Communist bureaucracy. He talked repeatedly about granting "sovereignty" to the union's republics, yet he never came up with a plan for freedom that appealed to the nationalist forces rising in all the republics. In the spring of 1990, when the Baltic republics insisted on their freedom, Gorbachev looked the other way as Soviet security forces moved in to suppress the independence movement. Even when the Communist party resorted to violence against him in the failed coup, Gorbachev publicly pledged his loyalty to that same party.

Perhaps the majority of the Soviet people were most dismayed by the fact that Gorbachev did not deliver on his promise that *perestroika* would bring efficiency to the socialist system and prosperity to the country. Under the Soviet system, the republics depended on each other economically. Following orders from the central government, factories in one republic obtained raw materials from other republics, and then supplied the manufactured products to the rest of the Soviet Union. This was, in theory, "all for one and one for all"; but in practice it was an ineffective system in which corruption reigned.

By 1990 the Communist party had begun to lose much of its power over the central government. And as communism lost favor, the fifteen union republics began to demand more control over their own affairs. When Communist control finally collapsed in 1991, the breakup of the Soviet Union was inevitable. The central government was no longer able to hold the republics together, and they entered a new era of independence and uncertainty.

Chapter 3

A Closer Look: The Founding Members

Russia, Belarus, and Ukraine together account for eighty percent of the former Soviet Union's territory and 211 million of its 290 million people. The three are known as the Slavic republics. As some of the biggest producers in manufacturing and agriculture, Russia, Belarus, and Ukraine naturally wield the most political power in the commonwealth.

The three Slavic republics account for most of the commonwealth's land and people.

Russia

Declared Independence: Did not formally declare
Population: 148,041,000
Area: 6,592,812 square miles (17,075,383 km²)
Capital and Largest City: Moscow (pop. 9,000,000)
Main Industries: Manufacturing (mining, machinery, textiles) and agriculture (livestock, grains)
Ethnic Composition: Russian 82%, Tartar 4%, Ukrainian 3%, other 11%

Russia never formally declared independence, but in 1990 the republic government declared that Russian laws took precedence over those of the Soviet Union.

Russia is a vast country, stretching from Eastern Europe across Asia to the Pacific Ocean and from the Arctic

Opposite:
Russian soldiers guard the Kremlin in Moscow. The Russian flag, which replaced the red flag of the Soviet Union, flies atop the Kremlin dome.

Ocean south to the Black Sea. It is the largest country in the world in terms of total area and the sixth largest in population.

Russia can be broken down into two regions: The urbanized west is the Russian state that was founded by Czar Ivan the Terrible and ruled by czars until 1917. Siberia is the vast eastern region that began to be conquered in 1581. Large-scale colonization began after the Trans-Siberian railroad was built in 1902. In the 1930s and 1940s, Siberia was the home of Stalin's infamous labor camps. While Siberia is rich in natural resources, the severe climate has hampered industrial development.

As the principal industrial and agricultural producer of the commonwealth, Russia since World War II has been one of the world's great economic powers. Today, with its economy in crisis, Russia is trying to make the painfully slow transition from state socialism to a free-market system like that of Western democracies.

The Free-Market System

Russia began a course known as "price liberalization" in January 1992. Price liberalization allows manufacturers, retailers, and regional authorities (rather than the central government) to set the price of most consumer goods and foods. Under communism, these prices were kept artificially low for decades. With price liberalization, however, prices have skyrocketed on everything from kindergarten to airplane tickets, and from beef to bricks.

It is still too early to decide the success or failure of Russian President Boris Yeltsin's policy of "crash capitalism." Soon after the coup, shops in Moscow filled up with foods that had been missing for months, like cheese, eggs, and meat. But, at the same time, prices rose tenfold or more. Most people have been learning to cope with the government's abrupt policy changes. While anxiety remains high, Russians are somehow managing to survive. They are digging deeper into cupboards stocked with reserves of macaroni, potatoes, and dry cereals. They are cutting back on purchases of shoes and furniture. And, in many cases, people are simply doing without. A fifty-two-

An elderly Russian woman wipes tears from her eyes as she waits to buy milk at 8 rubles per liter. Only months before, the price was 1.5 rubles per liter.

A sidewalk vendor in Moscow takes advantage of Russia's new free-market system by selling an assortment of Communist mementos to passersby.

year-old seamstress from Moscow explained to a *New York Times* reporter, "When we go into the shops, it's as if we are on an excursion. We come, we look, and we leave. Generally speaking, we live on bread and tea."

In step with the free-market rise in prices, salaries have also gone up. Russian miners, for example, recently won a six-fold wage increase. But mostly, wages lag far behind inflation. Government officials say that inflation is running at 250 percent, but critics say the figure is much higher than that.

Western investment is slowly building in Russia. In St. Petersburg, on weekends, children press their faces against the big glass window of Russia's first full-service Ford dealership.

"If it's slow, we invite them in," said salesman Sergei Golitinsky in an article in *Newsweek* magazine. "They sit in the cars with their eyes like this," he continued, forming big circles with his fingers. "They hold the steering wheel, and I think they are afraid to breathe."

Since Russia rid itself of communism, capitalists have turned from villains to heroes. A new foreign car has become the ultimate sign of success, but one that is not easily obtained. An average Russian worker earning about 1,000 rubles a month would have to save his or her entire salary for about eighty-three years to buy a no-frills Ford Escort for $10,000.

In Russia there is a growing romance with entrepreneurship—not only in the big cities, but in the provinces as well. Faced with dwindling prospects and pitiful salaries at their old state jobs, some Russians have launched themselves into an assortment of new endeavors. Commodity exchanges, radio stations, and advertising agencies are cropping up throughout Russia, in addition to other more ingenious ways of making a living.

A thirty-seven-year-old Moscow man named Sergei who directs a printing company told a *New York Times* reporter, "The only way to make ends meet is by working more intensively." He worked for a state factory until he set up his own business. Since he left government work, Sergei's salary has tripled. The average salary in the growing private sector is about 3,000 rubles per month. The unofficial national average is 800 to 1,000 rubles.

President Yeltsin announced a goal of having seventy-five percent of Russia's retail stores in private hands by the end of 1992. But there are many obstacles still to overcome. The Russian government has had to begin to address the problem of corruption in a new light. Many think that under democracy officials have become even greedier than they were under communism. Once the way of "greasing the wheels" in the slow-moving Communist bureaucracy, bribery has become part of the cost of doing business in a Russian democracy. More than ever before, it is a part of everyday life.

"I give bribes at every step," a store director said in a *New York Times* interview. "You can't get anything without bribes. I get a delivery of cigarettes—ten percent goes to the supplier, to the distributor. Looking for space for your store? That will be ten grand on top."

Hardline Communists demonstrated in Moscow during the winter of 1992 to protest rising prices, food shortages, and growing unemployment.

Other forms of corruption are also growing in popularity. Insider trading, Soviet style, is another common problem. Government officials with access to privileged economic information—for instance, on the availability of goods or property—share it with a select group of paying citizens. In other cases, well-placed officials and managers quietly strip away the best assets from failing state industries and form their own businesses.

Even with the many discouraging circumstances facing the average Russian, Yeltsin has warned about new difficulties and even harder times ahead. Yeltsin's own vice president, Alexander Rutskoi, has accused Russia's government of pursuing "economic genocide" against its own people. Still, Yeltsin's personal popularity remains the single most potent force behind the sweeping reforms. Although Yeltsin underwent some harsh criticism and organized opposition in March and April of 1992, his grip on Russia's government remained intact.

There were some demonstrations against high prices in the winter of 1991–92, but they were relatively small and limited to hardliners who want the old order restored. By and large, the demonstrations were ignored by a majority of the population.

Spiritual Revival

Russia is a nation undergoing spiritual rebirth as well as economic reform. The Russian Orthodox faith helped shape Russia from 988, when Prince Vladimir converted to Christianity, until 1917. Under communism, religion was officially banned. The faithful worshipped secretly and feared punishment. Mikhail Gorbachev lifted the Communist ban on worship in hopes that the church would become one of the building blocks for his reforms.

In a 1992 public opinion poll, a majority of Russians said they have found a sense of purpose and community in religion. Sanctuaries where once only a handful of older

A religious procession of Russian Orthodox priests passes by the Kremlin. With the death of communism came a great rebirth of religion in all the former Soviet Republics.

people prayed are now filled with worshippers of all ages. Priests perform baptisms and bless homes and even state office buildings. They perform weddings of couples who were married years earlier at state wedding palaces.

Right-wing nationalists have been accused of trying to exploit religion for their own ends, using their association with the church to give their hardline goals legitimacy. The anti-Semitic movement in Russia has also tried to identify itself with the Orthodox Church.

The re-emergence of anti-Semitism is one of the uglier aspects of change in Russia. Many Jews fear that they will be made scapegoats for the tough economic situation. They are also worried that gentiles resent the fact that Jews now enjoy a privileged position because they have a refuge, Israel, that is denied to everyone else. In fact, some gentiles are trying to pass themselves off as Jews in the hope of getting out of the country through Israel.

Because of the long Communist repression, no one is even sure how many Jews there are in the former Soviet Union. A Soviet government census in 1989 stated that there were 1.4 million, but other sources put the real number at closer to 3 million. Jews are rekindling traditions that were nearly wiped out by communism. Some Jews are beginning to identify themselves for the first time.

Jews are split in their assessment of the situation. Leonid Ashkinazi, a Moscow physicist, told a *New York Times* reporter, "Obviously, the situation is very unstable now and people are not very kind to each other. But Jews are not special on this point. When people stand on line at the shops, they don't say that the Jews are to blame. They say it's the Azerbaijanis or the Georgians or the Uzbeks, but not the Jews."

But Ashkinazi's wife, Mariya Gainer, disagreed, believing the chances are good that traditionally anti-Semitic nationalists or right-wingers will grab power. "The situation may not be so bad now for the Jews," she said "but the potential for it getting worse is big."

The Busy *Babushka*

Who in Russia minds the children after school, stands in line after line for hours to buy food and clothing, cooks meals, and even helps families during tough times by earning extra income? More than likely it's a *babushka*, or grandmother.

The babushka's contribution to Soviet society is not merely economic. For much of this century, she has also kept spiritual values alive. As Yevgenia Georgiyevna, a 71-year-old woman living in Moscow, told a *Newsweek* magazine reporter, ". . . babushkas have been alive practically since the revolution." They have "seen the good times and the bad times," she pointed out, and "know the difference between right and wrong." An office worker in Moscow probably spoke for many Russians when she told the same reporter, "The most important thing my babushka taught me is morality."

Communist doctrine discouraged family and religious ties, but the babushkas have become a social force despite and perhaps even because of the Soviet system. When women as well as men went to work under forced industrialization, young children were largely turned over to public day care centers. But a long workday created the need for someone to do especially time-consuming domestic chores. (Long shopping lines and households with few modern conveniences have been facts of Soviet life.) Babushkas were available to fill the need because of an early retirement age—55 for women—and an enduring extended family tradition. Since only 83,000 Russians live in retirement homes today—compared to over four million in the United States—Russian families often have a grandmother living with them or nearby.

And these babushkas have remained staunchly old-fashioned in at least one important sense: they have been Russia's largest group of churchgoers, even when open worship was punishable by the Soviet state. The religious devotion of an ever-present babushka was bound to affect the conscience of the Soviet family. Indeed, some believe that Mikhail Gorbachev was tolerant toward non-Communist beliefs and religious practice because of his own babushka. She had him baptized in the Russian Orthodox church in the 1930s—a time when the Communist prohibition against religion was especially severe.

The affectionate nickname *babushka* is actually a Slavic word for the kerchief that so many older Russian women wear on their heads.

A House Divided

There are twenty main subdivisions in the vast Russian federation that are essentially republics within the republic. Russia's nearly 150 million people include at least thirty-nine nationalities and scores of ethnic groups. Ethnic battles and resentment of Moscow's influence in the affairs of local governments have caused some groups to demand independence. The predominantly Muslim and oil-rich republic of Chechen-Ingush has declared independence, though without official recognition. Many in the Tartar republic also want independence. Like other ethnic minorities, the predominantly Muslim Tartars in the region (known as the Kazan Tartars) resent a history of "Russification," which deprived them of their language and their religion. The Bashkir republic has watched the Tartars carefully, sharing their concerns over Moscow's control of regional economic and natural resources.

President Yeltsin has said, "We want cooperation among the peoples of Russia to be built not on coercion and command but on freedom of choice and mutual benefit." The Russians have a long way to go before achieving such cooperation.

Ukraine

Declared Independence: August 24, 1991
Population: 51,839,000
Area: 233,089 square miles (603,700 km²)
Capital and Largest City: Kiev (pop. 2,616,000)
Main Industries: Agriculture (grains, dairy products) and manufacturing (electrical goods)
Ethnic Composition: Ukrainian 73%, Russian 22%, Jewish 1%, other 4%

Known as the "breadbasket" of the Soviet Union, Ukraine once accounted for twenty percent of Soviet agricultural output. Grain, potatoes, and dairy products make up most of the republic's agricultural products, while agricultural machinery and electrical appliances account for most of its industry. Located in southeastern Europe, the rich agricultural and industrial republic is second in economic size only to Russia.

Because of its agricultural and industrial importance, Ukraine's continued membership is considered vital to the commonwealth's success. But, like all other republics,

The Republic That Didn't Join

In 1991, rebels took up arms against the government of Georgian president Gamsakhurdia.

The former Soviet republic of Georgia has not joined the Commonwealth of Independent States. Fiercely nationalistic and independent, Georgians opted to remain separate from the new coalition.

Located in the Caucasus Mountains on the eastern shore of the Black Sea, Georgia is home to a proud mountain people who turned to Russia in 1801 for protection against the Turks and Persians. Georgia declared independence in 1918, but was militarily annexed by Stalin (who was born in Georgia) in 1921. In April 1991, Georgia once again declared its independence—this time, it hoped, for good.

Ethnic strife and political quarrels followed Georgian independence. Non-Communist president Zviad Gamsakhurdia's authoritarian style aroused intense opposition in the republic. In September 1991, the president's political opponents accused him of trying to establish a dictatorship and rose against him. A full-scale civil war broke out. President Gamsakhurdia was removed from office in January 1992.

Eduard Shevardnadze, a Georgian who served as Soviet foreign minister under Mikhail Gorbachev, returned to Georgia after seven years in Moscow to be chairman of a new top state body that hopes to map out the future of the republic.

Traditionally known for its tourist industry and active private sector, Georgia has a small but varied industry that has deteriorated as the republic's leadership neglected its economic affairs. With its moderate climate, Georgia cultivates crops not grown in most of the other republics, including tea and citrus fruits. It is also a popular vacation spot for many Russians.

Georgians claim to have produced more people who have lived to be over a hundred years of age than any other country in the world. It is not even that unusual to find 120-year-old Georgians! Like other peoples of the Caucasus known for their longevity, Georgians credit the clean mountain air and the vast quantities of yogurt they eat. The Georgians also cite the "positive effects" of their local brandy and wine.

Ukraine is riddled with growing pains. Economic reforms are stalled. Friction with Russia is growing. Ukraine hoped to avoid some of Russia's problems by issuing its own currency. But those hopes faded as the national currency diminished in value by more than ten times.

With oil supplies from Russia sharply curtailed, gasoline is sold illicitly by truck drivers for about sixty rubles per gallon—about fifteen times what the price would be at the pumps, if the pumps had any. Natural gas from the republic of Turkmenistan, the major supplier to Ukrainian industry, was halted over a price dispute. Moreover, miners all over Ukraine are complaining about wages.

Wrangling between Ukraine and the Russian republic over defense issues has greatly disrupted the cooperative efforts of the Commonwealth of Independent States. The

A Ukrainian woman displays a wide variety of produce at an outdoor market at Lvov. Unlike many of the other republics, Ukraine maintains a productive agricultural base.

driving force behind the disputes is the perception among Ukrainians that the largest republic is a huge and immediate threat, a hungry imperialist power fundamentally incapable of accepting Ukrainian independence.

In 1991, Ukraine pledged to eliminate all nuclear weapons based on its territory by 1994, shipping them to Russia for dismantling. It later halted shipments, fearing that the Russians wouldn't actually destroy the arms, but resumed them in 1992. (The strategic, or long-range, nuclear arms in Ukraine included 176 intercontinental ballistic missiles capable of reaching the United States.) Ukraine also claimed the former Soviet Black Sea fleet as its own, but Russia wanted to control the naval force. Tensions between Ukraine and Russia heightened in May 1992, when the pro-Russian Crimean Parliament voted to declare their own conditional independence from Ukraine. Crimea, which is home to the Black Sea fleet, belonged to Russia before Nikita Khrushchev "gave" it to Ukraine as a gift of solidarity.

To understand Ukrainian fear of the Russians it is helpful to understand some of the history of the country.

Soviet economic control of the republics left their economies in ruins after the collapse of communism. Here, a homeless man sleeps in a square in Kiev near a statue of Vladimir Lenin.

The Russians gained control over most of Ukraine in 1795, imposing a life of serfdom on Ukrainians. The people resented the harsh way of life and the czar's efforts to replace the Ukrainian language with Russian. Then, with Communist rule, the government began to take control of small peasant farms. In 1929, Stalin forced most of the country's peasants onto collective farms. When the peasants resisted, millions of the more prosperous farmers were stripped of their property and exiled to Siberia. The Communists wiped out lingering defiance through a deliberate "terror famine" in 1932. Millions of people died of starvation. "A single death is a tragedy, a million deaths is a statistic," Stalin was quoted as saying.

Ukrainian distrust of Russian government was reinforced in 1986 when a fire and explosion at the nuclear power plant in Chernobyl, near Kiev, released large amounts of radioactive material into the atmosphere. Soviet officials reported that thirty-one people died and over two hundred were seriously injured. Ukrainians believed that the casualties were much higher and that thousands were exposed to dangerous levels of radiation.

When Ukrainians voted for independence they did so with expectations of a better life. In some ways, life in Ukraine has improved with independence. Citizens seem to enjoy a new pride in speaking their native Ukrainian, which is related to Russian. And as uncomfortable as the shortages and higher prices have been, there is still far more food in the markets of Kiev than there is in the markets of Moscow.

While embracing democratic principles, Ukrainians are concerned foremost with building their state and sorting out their economy. Many Ukrainians see the new commonwealth as only a temporary mechanism for the peaceful dissolution of the Soviet Union—not, as the Russians are apt to view it, as a permanent association. Many Ukrainians believe (and even hope) that the newly created commonwealth will eventually disappear.

Belarus (Byelorussia)

Declared Independence: August 25, 1991
Population: 10,259,000
Area: 80,151 square miles (207,590 km^2)
Capital and Largest City: Minsk (pop. 1,613,000)
Main Industries: Agriculture (dairy products) and
    manufacturing (electrical appliances)
Ethnic Composition: Byelorussian 78%, Russian 13%,
    Polish 4%, other 5%

Belarus, a nation of ten million people, is sometimes referred to as "the most quiet republic." Minsk, its capital, is also the headquarters of the new commonwealth. Long considered the most conservative of the Slavic republics, Belarus has a tortured history. During the 1930s, the Stalinist purges took a bitter and devastating toll on the people and spirit of the republic.

Belarus musicians entertaining citizens of Minsk in the city's downtown area.

A trip to Kuropaty Forest, about five miles northeast of Minsk, reveals a haunting site. Hidden by a pine forest are acre upon acre of graves. Henrick Smith, in *The New Russians,* quotes a local guide on what happened in Belarus during Stalin's reign of terror: "Over the course of four and a half years, they shot people here every day. Literally every day. . . . People were taken out of trucks. Their hands were untied. Secret police officers stood around the 'grave' pits—revolvers ready so that no one could run away. Pairs were led up to the pits and shot in the back of the head. Usually people, when they were untied, understood that they had been brought to be killed. They threw themselves on their knees and usually asked why they were being killed. They appealed to God, prayed, and remembered their families."

From 1937 to 1941, Stalin ordered the annihilation of Byelorussian farmers and intelligentsia in an attempt to "Russify" the country and entrench communism in the entire region. Mass murders were conducted not only in Kuropaty Forest, but all over the republic.

Republic leaders meet in Minsk, which was declared the official capital of the Commonwealth of Independent States.

Today, although the Belarus people share many cultural similarities with their Russian neighbors, including a related language, they are also ardently protective of their identity as separate from other republics. The decision to locate the commonwealth's capital in Minsk was, in part, a symbolic act, clearing the slate of Moscow's structures and bureaucracy. Embracing democratic principles, Belarus is working hard to make an easy transition to free markets from state control of the economy. Belarus is one of the commonwealth's most productive republics, with factories and mills turning out cars, bicycles, farm machinery, TV sets, textiles, cement, steel, and lumber.

One of the most pressing challenges facing Belarus has been coping with the damage done by the Chernobyl nuclear plant accident. Estimates are that seventy percent of the radiation fell on Belarus, contaminating one-fifth of its farmable land, where two million people live.

Chapter 4

The Other Commonwealth Members

There are eight other former Soviet republics: Moldova, Armenia, Azerbaijan, and the Central Asian republics of Kazakhstan, Uzbekistan, Turkmenistan, Tajikistan, and Kyrgyzstan. Their names are unfamiliar to many people in the West; so are the republics themselves. Yet all are struggling to take a place on the world stage.

Moldova (Moldavia)

Declared Independence: August 27, 1991
Population: 4,362,000
Area: 13,000 square miles (33,670 km²)
Capital and Largest City: Kishinev (pop. 676,000)
Main Industry: Agriculture (grapes)
Ethnic Composition: Moldovan 64%, Ukrainian 14%, Russian 13%, other 9%

Once part of Romania, Moldova was incorporated into the Soviet Union in 1924 (the western part) and in 1940. In language, culture, and ethnic background, Moldovans are basically indistinguishable from Romanians. But over the years there were strong attempts to "Russify" the republic.

Communist authorities tried to replace Moldovan with Russian as the language to be used in schools. Moldovan

Eight other republics enjoy the freedom of new societies but struggle with the challenges of independence.

Opposite:
A Moldovan farmer wears the typical dress of Moldova's countryside.

theaters, libraries, orchestras, museums, the academy of sciences, and other cultural activities—with the exception of folk music and dance—were run by non-Moldovans. In effect, Moldovans have historically been an underprivileged majority in their own country.

Moldova's ethnic Romanian majority is increasingly nationalistic today. Many want to reunify with neighboring Romania. "We are Romanians first and Moldovans second," said one Moldovan.

Russians and Ukrainians living in the Dniester region of Moldova are extremely uncomfortable with the Romanian influence. The "Dniester Moldovan Republic," whose 600,000 Russians and Ukrainians fear reunification with Romania, wants to have its own separate government.

Moldova is struggling with many of the economic problems that other republics face. Moldova's economy depends mainly on farming and food processing. Known primarily for its grapes and wine, Moldova also has a small manufacturing base that produces shoes, clothing, and electrical appliances. The republic imports all of its coal, natural gas, and oil—mostly from Ukraine and Russia.

Armenia

Declared Independence: September 23, 1991
Population: 3,293,000
Area: 11,500 square miles (29,785 km^2)
Main Industries: Agriculture and manufacturing
Capital and Largest City: Yerevan (pop. 1,202,000)
Ethnic Composition: Armenian 93%, Russian 2%,
   other 5%

Armenia lies south of the Caucasus mountains in Asia. After a brief period of independence in 1917, Armenia sought Russia's protection from the Turks and formed a Soviet republic in 1920. Today, most of the people live in cities and work in industry, but some farm or raise livestock for a living. Armenian farmers produce mostly fruit and wine grapes, while the republic's industry focuses primarily on clothing and textiles.

Most Armenians are Christians and belong to the Armenian Church, an eastern orthodox church. In addition to being generally religious, Armenians also place importance on hospitality and close family ties. They try to instill in their children a love for Armenian traditions.

In 1990, non-Communists won control over Armenia's government. The republic's legislature adopted a declaration stating that Armenia's laws took precedence over Soviet laws. The legislature then called for gradual separation from the Soviet Union. In September 1991, the majority of Armenians voted in favor of independence.

Armenian dancers dress in brightly colored native costumes for a celebration of independence.

In Armenia, the absence of Soviet repression has also led to violence. Since 1988, the republic has been embroiled in a territorial dispute with neighboring Azerbaijan. In 1991, that dispute turned bloody, with Armenian and Azerbaijan troops battling each other in various parts of both republics.

Azerbaijan

Declared Independence: August 30, 1991
Population: 7,081,000
Area: 33,400 square miles (86,506 km²)
Capital and Largest City: Baku (pop. 1,780,000)
Main Industry: Oil
Ethnic Composition: Azeri 83%, Russian 6%,
    Armenian 6%, other 5%

Azerbaijan, on the western shore of the Caspian Sea, was under strict control by the Soviet Union's central government since the 1930s, when Soviet leaders revived their efforts to suppress non-Russian cultures.

The unraveling of Communist authority was particularly dramatic in Azerbaijan. Toward the end of 1988, a group of intellectuals in the capital city of Baku started to set up a democratic-style popular front to promote political and

A Bloody Dispute

In 1988, large numbers of Armenians demonstrated in their capital city of Yerevan and in other cities. They demanded that a district of the neighboring republic of Azerbaijan be made a part of Armenia. Most of the people who live in the district, called Nagorno-Karabakh, are Armenian Christians. A small minority are Muslims.

In the beginning, the Soviet government rejected the Armenian demand and tried to maintain the status quo. As demonstrations in the region intensified, they led to the flight of thousands of frightened Azeris. On the other side, rumors of atrocities by Armenians led to the killings of dozens of Armenians in Azerbaijan. Then, in the spring of 1991, Soviet and Azeri troops joined in a disastrous campaign to drive Armenians from the villages of Nagorno-Karabakh.

After the failed Moscow coup attempt in August 1991, President Yeltsin tried to mediate the Azerbaijan/Armenia dispute but failed miserably. With the USSR in ruins, Soviet troops pulled out of the region and the tide turned in favor of the Armenians, who began driving the Azeris from Nagorno-Karabakh.

By early 1992, an estimated two thousand people had died in this conflict. But the misery went far beyond the killing. The Armenians of Nagorno-Karabakh had essentially been cut off from the outside world, supplied with food and goods only by helicopter. The entire republic of Armenia suffered through a winter without heat because the Azeris cut off its oil supply.

As the killing went on, peace talks continued. Numerous cease-fire agreements collapsed during the four year struggle. A cease-fire agreed to in March 1992 was shattered within hours as shelling continued in Nagorno-Karabakh. Since that time, Armenia and Azerbaijan have asked the United Nations to help them resolve the dispute.

A young boy cradles his rifle at the funeral for a man killed in the fighting over Nagorno-Karabakh.

economic reform. The Azeris were disgusted with their economic situation, environmental pollution, corrupt local leadership, and exploitation by the Soviet system. For example, Moscow bought oil from Azerbaijan at a small fraction of the world market price. Azeris knew that unfair advantage was being taken and this fueled their grass-roots movement toward independence.

As a predominantly Shiite Muslim society, Azerbaijan has close ties to Iran. Its territorial clashes with Armenia date back to the late 1980s.

Oil is Azerbaijan's chief source of wealth. The capital city of Baku has an impressive concentration of oil refineries. Other mineral resources are iron, aluminum ore, and cobalt. Azerbaijan's small industries produce steel pipes for the oil industry, textiles, and such home appliances as refrigerators.

Located in the southern Caucasus Mountains, Azerbaijan's highlands are used primarily for grazing. Fisheries on the Caspian Sea produce carp and sturgeon, caviar and canned products. Farmers in Azerbaijan's fertile and productive lowlands produce corn, cotton, fruits, teas, rice, vegetables, tobacco, and walnuts.

The Central Asian Republics

For centuries before they were conquered by the Russian Empire, the five Central Asian republics of Kazakhstan, Uzbekistan, Turkmenistan, Tajikistan, and Kyrgyzstan were collectively known as Turkestan. It was in Turkestan that a rich and sophisticated Islamic civilization was nurtured by great trade routes from China that ran through Tashkent and the region's other major cities. The old Silk Road, which ran across Asia, served as a cultural bridge between East and West. From the tenth through fifteenth centuries, this busy and highly developed trade route brought a rich mix of political, social, and religious customs to the region.

Today, almost nothing of Turkestan's great civilization remains. When Vladimir Lenin and the Bolsheviks took control of Moscow during the Russian revolution of 1917, they began a campaign of brutal oppression that would, by the early 1920s, reach the republics of Central Asia. The purpose of their campaign was to "Russify" all of the Soviet Union's republics and to erase all non-Communist influence from the region. By 1925, Joseph Stalin had carved up Central Asia into five republics, erasing the name Turkestan from the map and suppressing the region's rich culture.

Stalin's domination had far-reaching, visible, and very painful effects. Many examples of Turkestan's grandest architecture were torn down and replaced by plain buildings designed to serve purely utilitarian purposes. Also, communist doctrine required that religion be erased from

society entirely. For the millions of Muslims of central Asia, this meant that the cornerstone of their culture—the practice of Islam—would be severely punished. Public rituals and Islamic cultural displays were banned in favor of activities that glorified the Communist party.

The Soviet Union included the fifth-largest Islamic population in the world, enveloping more than sixty million Muslims. When the Soviet Union self-destructed in August 1991, new life was breathed into the Central Asian republics, particularly for devout Muslims. Suddenly, the bleak restrictions of Communist rule were lifted and the people became free to publicly reclaim their own identities and cultures. With that freedom came a great resurgence of Islam.

The Muslims of Central Asia differ somewhat from their neighbors in Iran. The majority of Muslims in Iran are Shiite, while the majority in Central Asia are Sunni Muslim. In Shiism—commonly thought to be the "stricter" of the two branches of Islam—the clergy are called upon to intercede between God and humans. This makes the Shiite clergy (known as *mullahs* and *imams*) very powerful voices in their society. The Sunnis, however, believe that humans have a direct relationship with God, and clergy are mostly useful as advisers or spiritual guides.

Today, the influence and rebirth of Islam can be seen almost everywhere in the five Asian republics. Some estimates claim that Central Asia now opens an average of ten new mosques a day. Abdullah Ismailov, chief of the Uzbekistan Directorate's international department, explained the dimensions of Islam's growth to a writer for *The New Yorker*: "Three years ago, there were about eighty mosques in Uzbekistan. Now in the Namangan region alone there are more than a thousand, and Namangan is only one of twelve Uzbek regions."

As Islam continues to play an increasingly large role in each of the five republics, new questions emerge. Most specifically, how will Islam be integrated into Central

Opposite:
Uzbekistan's faithful gather for a prayer at a mosque in Termez.

Uzbekistan

Declared Independence: August 31, 1991
Population: 20,322,000
Area: 172,700 square miles (447,293 km²)
Capital and Largest City: Tashkent (pop. 2,094,000)
Main Industry: Agriculture (cotton)
Ethnic Composition: Uzbek 71%, Russian 8%, Tajik 5%, other 16%

Kazakhstan

Declared Independence: Did not formally declare
Population: 16,691,000
Area: 1,049,155 square miles (2,717,311 km²)
Capital and Largest City: Alma-Ata (pop. 2,094,000)
Main Industry: Agriculture (livestock), and manufacturing (mining)
Ethnic Composition: Kazakh 40%, Russian 38%, German 6%, Slav 7%, other 9%

Turkmenistan (Turkmenia)

Declared Independence: October 27, 1991
Population: 3,622,000
Area: 188,456 square miles (488,101 km²)
Capital and Largest City: Ashkhabad (pop. 407,000)
Main Industry: Agriculture (livestock and cotton)
Ethnic Composition: Turkmen 72%, Russian 9%, Uzbek 9%, other 10%

Kyrgyzstan (Kirghizia)

Declared Independence: August 31, 1991
Population: 4,367,000
Area: 76,641 square miles (198,500 km²)
Capital and Largest City: Bishkek (formerly Frunze; pop. 616,000)
Main Industry: Agriculture (livestock), and manufacturing (mining)
Ethnic Composition: Kyrgyz 52%, Russian 21%, Uzbek 13%, other 14%

Tajikistan (Tadzhikistan)

Declared Independence: September 9, 1991
Population: 5,248,000
Area: 55,251 square miles (143,100 km²)
Capital and Largest City: Dushanbe (pop. 602,000)
Main Industry: Agriculture (cotton)
Ethnic Composition: Tajik 62%, Uzbek 24%, Russian 8%, other 6%

Asia's new governments and policies? This is the fundamental question faced by each of the five republics. Each republic, however, has differing opinions about the role that Islam should play in future governments.

The Idea of a New Turkestan

As the debate continues, proposals for a new Turkestan gain in popularity. Many believe a new Turkestan would rejuvenate the glory of the republics' lost heritage. But the question of just how Turkestan would be constructed is still not clear. Some republics favor a loose confederation that would serve to consolidate the resources of the five republics for economic gain, much in the same manner of the newly launched European Community. Others hope to make Turkestan a more rigid state, with a central administration and a central body of laws.

In Uzbekistan and Kazakhstan, many people envision Turkestan as a modern cultural and economic community that would incorporate aspects of many different cultures and beliefs. In a *New Yorker* article, Jamal Kamal, one of Uzbekistan's most famous writers, asserts that, "Turkestan will not be one solid, united state. Uzbekistan, Tajikistan, and the others will continue. Each will still have its own name. Turkestan will be more like an economic and cultural federation. Maybe only after many years will it become one state." Other Uzbek government officials elaborated on Kamal's description. They stressed their belief that Turkestan will not be an exclusively Islamic state. "The model is Turkey," one official explained. "The state is secular and has modern industry and connections with both Europe and Asia."

In Tajikistan—where nationalistic and religious forces come closest together—few favor the idea of Turkestan. There are strong elements in Tajikistan that support the eventual creation of an Islamic state, but one that would remain in touch with the modern nations of Europe and the West. Other forces favor a more democratically based

A Kyrgyz mother comforts her children after ethnic violence in Bishkek destroyed homes and left many dead.

government. Conflicts between pro-Islamic forces erupted in violence in May 1992. In the capital city of Dushanbe, at least fourteen people were killed and many were wounded in a bloody confrontation. Tajikistan's most powerful religious leader, known as the Qazi, is strongly opposed to the creation of Turkestan and a pro-democracy government. He supports close relations with Islamic countries such as Iran and Afghanistan. "We are united by more than a thousand years of history," he told a *New Yorker* writer.

In Kyrgyzstan, the vision of Turkestan takes on yet another form. Kyrgyzstan, the most democratic of the Central Asian republics, was the first newly independent state to hold free national presidential elections. In this republic, the citizens have already come a long way toward aligning themselves with the democracies and multi-party systems of Europe and the West. For the Kyrgyz, a newly unified Turkestan would have to be loose enough and democratic enough to allow their republic's progress toward a free-market economy to remain intact.

Even though there is strong sentiment for an Islamic-influenced society throughout the republics, most of the region's people agree that certain elements of democracy and a free-market system must play a part in their future governments. These are elements that most feel are necessary for economic survival. The Asian republics have seen in Iran a more fanatical model of an Islamic government. They have seen isolationist policies that have effectively deprived Iranians of many benefits of the modern world.

Economic Reform

Most citizens in the Central Asian republics realize that their politics must be colored by economics. With their economies in ruins, the Asian republics cannot afford to cut themselves off from the global community. Instead, they need to foster ties with prosperous nations.

As part of the Soviet Union, the economies of the five republics were controlled completely by Moscow. Agricultural production was dictated by the Kremlin, as were the prices to be paid for crops. Some of the crops that were grown had been in place for over 130 years. When the Civil War in America cut off supplies of cotton to Russia in the 1860s, the czars looked to their Asian colony for help. By the time Stalin took control of the government, the five republics had increasingly been assigned the task of growing cotton for the USSR. By the early 1980s, the cotton crop of Uzbekistan alone almost matched that of the United States. Production in the five republics was great enough to make cotton one of the USSR's major exports, which it shipped to over thirty countries.

With the collapse of the Soviet Union came the virtual collapse of the Central Asian economies. Whereas they were previously controlled and protected by the Soviet

Uzbek laborers work in the cotton fields. Cotton production dominated the economies of all the Central Asian republics under Soviet rule.

government, after the coup the republics were suddenly faced with fending for themselves. And they did not have much to work with. In 1989, figures showed that the Central Asian republics were the poorest of the USSR. The annual per capita income in Uzbekistan was less than half of Russia's. To add to their problems, too much of the republics' resources and labor force were dedicated solely to one crop, cotton. In Uzbekistan, cotton production accounts for forty percent of the labor force and consumes sixty percent of the republic's resources.

In addition to the crippling effects of the cotton-based economy, the republics also face the consequences of decades of irresponsible and reckless Soviet management. Because they ignored the importance of crop rotation, the Soviets severely depleted the region's once-fertile soil of its nutrients. Years of unchecked pesticide use now cause great concern over the potential health risks for both humans and animals in the region. Reckless drainage of rivers and lakes for irrigation has caused many natural resources to deteriorate drastically. The Aral Sea—once the world's fourth-largest inland lake—has shrunk to sixty percent of its former size because two of its major tributaries were diverted for cotton irrigation.

Because their environment and economies are so severely threatened, the five republics have already begun to take steps toward greater economic self-sufficiency. A week before the August coup, the Central Asian republics agreed to form a Central Asian common market that would effectively reduce trade barriers among them. Then, a few months after the coup, the Central Asian republics joined the Commonwealth of Independent States in an effort to further good relations among all former Soviet republics. In February 1992, Uzbekistan, Turkmenistan, Tajikistan, and Kyrgyzstan joined with Iran, Turkey, and Pakistan to form an Islamic common market (Kazakhstan remained an "observer"). The effects of these coalitions are yet to be seen.

Kazakhstan's president, Nursultan Nazarbayev, controls one of the commonwealth's most important nuclear arsenals.

The Soviet Legacy: Environmental Disaster

Nations the world over are now facing serious environmental problems created in the name of progress. The Commonwealth of Independent States, however, has inherited a level of environmental destruction unmatched anywhere—a tragic legacy of Soviet rule. In its single-minded determination to turn an agrarian society into a major industrial nation, the USSR polluted its air, water, land, and—finally—its people with the toxic waste of industry and urbanization.

The commonwealth's most deadly pollutants are its aging network of nuclear power plants. Radioactive material released in Chernobyl has contaminated more than 50,000 square miles of Ukraine's most fertile soil and hundreds of tons of livestock, and caused countless human illnesses and death.

Alexei Yablokov, President Yeltsin's science advisor, told a writer for *U.S. News & World Report* that "every nuclear power station is in no-good condition, a lot of leaks." In 1991, there were 270 recorded malfunctions at nuclear facilities, with at least 16 plants threatening to leak. But Russia, which relies heavily on nuclear power to generate electricity, lacks the resources to convert to other kinds of power.

Not all radiation has been caused by accident, however. According to *U.S. News & World Report*, a previously unreleased Soviet radiation map marks more than 130 nuclear explosions, carried out mostly in European Russia. The map also marks two offshore areas where nuclear reactors and radioactive waste were dumped into the sea. Because the Soviet government kept this information secret, no one knows how much land, water, and wildlife were contaminated, nor what their effect on human life will be.

Two other major destroyers of the Russian environment have been manufacturing and agriculture. Mills and processing plants have been releasing toxic chemicals into the air and dumping them into bodies of water for years. In 103 cities, Russians breathe air that exceeds five times the allowable pollution limits. Respiratory illnesses have become widespread in some industrial cities, especially afflicting children.

Acid rain caused by oil processing and reckless cutting has been destroying about five million acres of Siberian forestland a year. The Volga River and the Baltic Sea are seriously polluted by toxic waste and untreated sewage. Unecological farming methods, including the heavy use of pesticides, have poisoned or eroded vast amounts of farmland.

Until the commonwealth's economy improves enough to make its citizens turn their attention to the environment rather than their livelihood, there is little hope of improvement in this bleak picture.

A Place in the Commonwealth

As members of the Commonwealth of Independent States, the Central Asian republics hope to join with other ex-Soviet republics for economic support and cooperation. For some, such as the small and remote republic of Tajikistan, economic cooperation is crucial to survival. More than ninety-five percent of Tajikistan's land is unproductive desert. Without the support of other republics, Tajikistan would perish. Turkmenistan, too, contains largely non-farmable land. It is ninety percent desert.

Although the Asian republics seemed to have been largely ignored by the Soviet regime, the new commonwealth can no longer consider them any less important than the European republics. Kazakhstan—in size alone—is larger than all the other non-Russian republics combined. (Indeed, Kazakhstan is larger than Western Europe). It also houses a formidable nuclear arsenal that is yet another legacy of Soviet domination. Kazakhstan produces almost one-fifth of the coal that is mined in the commonwealth region and possesses immense but untapped oil reserves and other valuable resources.

Uzbekistan, with its population of twenty million, has the third largest population in the commonwealth (surpassed only by Russia and Ukraine). Altogether, the population of the Asian republics is one of their greatest assets. Between 1960 and 1980, the Asian population of the USSR grew almost four times faster than that of Russia. In addition, the republics of Turkmenistan, Kyrgyzstan, and Tajikistan—though relatively small—possess some natural resources and industry that can serve the commonwealth well. Each also has a border with non-commonwealth countries, making these republics strategically important for national security.

The future of Turkestan and the role that the Central Asian republics will play in the commonwealth and the world are still not known. Clearly, the lure of democracy and a free-market economy will continue to complicate the debate over how much Islam should rule the region.

A family of rugmakers works in a shop in Tajikistan.

Soviet Cosmonauts as Rip Van Winkles

Remember the story of Rip Van Winkle? He was the man who, after a long sleep, awoke to find his entire world had changed. Two Soviet cosmonauts are modern day Rip Van Winkles. Cosmonauts Sergei Krikalev and Alexander Volkov came back to Earth to find the world forever changed as well.

While circling Earth for ten months on the Mir space station, Krikalev watched helplessly as the Soviet Union fought off a coup, changed leaders, and then went out of existence. Even his hometown changed its name while he was in space. Krikalev came from Leningrad, which decided to take back its former name, St. Petersburg.

The situation for Krikalev's comrade, Aleksander Volkov, was a complicated one as well. He had arrived to command the orbiting space station five months after Krikalev, who was sent up on May 18, 1991. Volkov was born in Ukraine. Chilly relations between Russia and his home republic made Volkov's status as a cosmonaut shaky.

Financial problems forced a delay in the cosmonauts' retrieval from space. Glavkosmos, the Russian space agency, could barely afford to send supplies to Mir. And with the breakup of the Soviet Union, Russia and Kazakhstan began to fight over how to administer the huge Baikonur Cosmodrome, which is in Kazakhstan. Kazakhstan's government tried to charge massive fees for use of the space complex, and Russia—already strapped for funds—worked out a deal to launch the first Kazakh cosmonaut in return for easier access to the cosmodrome. The agreement caused another delay because the Kazakh cosmonaut was not experienced enough to replace Krikalev as flight engineer aboard Mir.

Originally scheduled to return in October 1991, Krikalev and Volkov continued to spin around Earth sixteen times a day while economic, territorial, and bureaucratic battles waged down below.

Finally, on March 25, 1992, Krikalev and Volkov returned to Earth at the Baikonur Cosmodrome. This has been the site of all Soviet manned launches since 1961, when Yuri Gagarin became the first person to soar into space. But the cosmodrome was not the same place it had been when the cosmonauts left. The future of the former Soviet space program—like the future of the republics—was unclear. Designed to house up to twelve cosmonauts, the huge Mir station had been manned almost continuously since 1986. It was the focal point of the Soviet space program. Some experts say the station is now nearing the end of its usefulness and must be either modernized or destroyed.

Krikalev, however, remained optimistic that he would eventually learn to live in his new environment. "In order to understand everything and get used to it, it is necessary to return and plunge into life," Krikalev was quoted as saying by the Australian Associated Press.

Each of these five unique republics will continue to search for its proper identity in the new world that has been created around them. A Tajik filmmaker, speaking to a *New Yorker* writer, described the future of the Central Asian republics this way: "Each republic has its own way to democracy, but the main task for each is to undo the years of tension that communism has imposed on us and to organize an orderly transition, so the republics don't unravel under conflicting pressures. Our goal during the transition has to be civil peace. But that's difficult to come by, in real life or in the movies."

Chapter 5

What the Future Holds

With the Commonwealth of Independent States groping to find new economic, political, and military paths, the world community was dealing with separate states, four of which were nuclear powers and most of which were unstable. Politicians and diplomats tried to predict what the post-Soviet era would mean for international relations. The United States and its allies have struggled to come up with new policies toward the former Soviet republics and their wobbly Commonwealth of Independent States. So far, the West has concentrated its efforts on the Russian republic.

A New Partnership for Old Rivals

On February 1, 1992, Boris Yeltsin spent more than three hours with George Bush at Camp David, the presidential hideaway in the Maryland mountains that has hosted a number of historic meetings. Together, the American and Russian presidents declared an end to the Cold War. They proclaimed a new era of "friendship and partnership" and declared a formal end to decades of rivalry.

The Camp David Declaration outlined general principles for relations between the United States and Russia. "Russia and the United States do not regard each other as

Will cooperation and compromise prevail despite longstanding hostilities between the republics?

Opposite:
U.S. President George Bush and Boris Yeltsin met at Camp David in February 1992. Their meeting established new guidelines for cooperation between Russia and the United States.

potential adversaries," the declaration said. "From now on, the relationship will be characterized by friendship and partnership founded in mutual trust and respect and a common commitment to democracy and economic freedom." Such words signaled a dramatic change in relations.

President Yeltsin said, "Today one might say that there has been written and drawn a new line, and crossed out all of the things that have been associated with the Cold War.

"From now on, we do not consider ourselves to be potential enemies, as it has been previously in our military doctrine. This is the historic value of this meeting. . . . In the future there'll be full frankness, full openness, full honesty in our relationship."

A Question of Aid

At Camp David, President Bush was strongly supportive of Yeltsin's political and economic reforms. He said he was "totally convinced" of Russia's commitment to democracy and hoped to assist "in any way possible."

But Yeltsin said that his country needed far more than money if it was to make a successful transition to democracy. "I didn't come here just to stretch out my hand and ask for help," the Russian leader said. "No, we're calling for a cooperation for the whole world, because if the reform in Russia goes under, that means there will be a cold war. The cold war is going to turn into a hot war. This is, again, going to be an arms race."

In the months that followed this historic meeting, President Bush was criticized for not doing enough to aid Russia. Former President Richard Nixon was one of Bush's loudest critics. But in April 1992, President Bush made a formal pledge to provide more substantial aid to the Commonwealth of Independent States. Bush announced that the United States would provide about one-fifth of a $24 billion multinational aid package for Russia. The $24 billion in assistance would include a $6 billion

Richard Nixon has been a vocal proponent of increased aid to the Commonwealth of Independent States.

fund to stabilize the ruble, $2.5 in debt rescheduling, $4.5 billion in loans from the International Monetary Fund and other organizations, and some $11 billion in direct help from Washington and other industrialized democracies that would include food, medicine, and export credits.

President Bush said Americans stood at a moment as important to twentieth century history as the ends of the two World Wars. America, he pointed out, had the chance to turn political chaos into lasting peace by adding a few billion dollars to the trillions it cost to wage the Cold War.

"The stakes are as high for us now as any we have faced in this century," Bush said at a White House news conference. "Our adversary for forty-five years, the one nation that posed a worldwide threat to freedom and peace, is now seeking to join the community of free nations."

Weapons in a New Light

The end of the Cold War has left the United States wondering how many weapons it now needs. In the past, America's nuclear planners worried about deterring a massive and powerful empire. Now the weapons of the former USSR are spread out in independent republics. All of the long-range nuclear weapons in the former Soviet arsenal are located in the republics of Russia, Ukraine, Belarus, and Kazakhstan. These are the weapons with the greatest destructive potential to the United States.

In June 1992, Boris Yeltsin made a visit to Washington, D.C., this time to meet with President Bush on the subject of mutual reductions in nuclear weapons. Secretary of State James Baker spent days in talks with Russian Foreign Minister Andrei Kozyrev to prepare for the Bush-Yeltsin meeting. By the time Yeltsin arrived in Washington on June 16, both sides had agreed on many fundamental points. It remained only for the two leaders to announce the actual scope of their accord to the rest of the world. Later that day, Yeltsin and Bush announced a major agreement that would sharply reduce long-range and multiple warhead missiles between both countries. "With this agreement," Bush announced, "the nuclear nightmare recedes more and more for ourselves, for our children, and for our grandchildren."

Although there have been many reductions, the three-million-troop ex-Soviet military, down from five million, is still the largest military force in the world. Russia has told the United States that it intends to maintain a smaller military force than Washington expected, keeping approximately 1.3 million troops in its armed forces and assigning the troops more defensive positions.

But the collapse of the USSR has caused morale among the troops to plummet. Soldiers in what was formerly the Leningrad Military District built pigsties and planted vegetable gardens so they would be assured of having

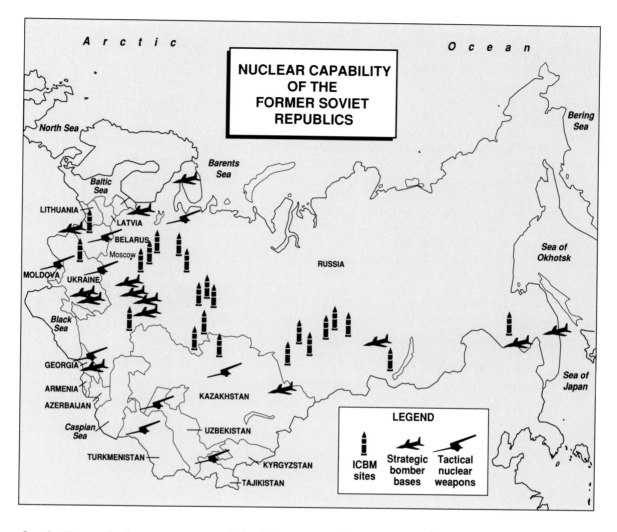

food. Barracks have run out of clothing, as well as medical supplies, gasoline, and parachutes.

More than ten thousand officers' families in Moscow lack homes of their own. Officers stationed in Ukraine set up housekeeping in a stable. Officers no longer have access to special stores, travel abroad, and choice apartments. Wages are being battered by inflation. A Soviet soldier earns seven rubles a month, while a kilo (about two pounds) of sausage costs eighty-seven rubles. "What do you expect of an army if a colonel—a colonel!—is paid less than a bus driver?" asked an officer in a *Time* magazine article.

Genius for Hire:
The Market for Soviet Scientists

With the Cold War declared over, the once enormous Soviet defense industry has been closing down. When the commonwealth announced major cuts in military projects in 1992, many Soviet scientists and engineers lost their jobs. Some left to work in the West. Those who were lucky enough to still be working at home were moonlighting to make ends meet. Their once respectable salaries—1,500 rubles for a top nuclear bomb designer—bought less and less as the ruble lost value.

But unlike other commonwealth citizens who were desperate to earn a livelihood, Soviet scientists were keenly aware of their value to the world. They had been feared and respected for their sophistication in mathematical and nuclear sciences. They also knew that the United States in particular was concerned that hostile nations might benefit from Soviet expertise in nuclear science.

In February 1992, a group of top scientists at a military nuclear complex, Chelyabinsk-70, invited U.S. Secretary of State James Baker to the once-secret facility. If the West would invest in them, they said, they could apply their considerable expertise to producing non-military products, such as industrial diamonds, fiber-optical and nuclear medical equipment, and computer software.

Also in 1992, a team of over one thousand nuclear fusion scientists at the Kurchatov Institute of Atomic Energy in Moscow signed a contract to work for the United States government. Their services would cost American taxpayers a mere $90,000.

In his Camp David meeting with Boris Yeltsin, President Bush discussed setting up a joint Russian-American research center where Russian nuclear scientists would collaborate on projects with American scientists.

America's scientific community was enthusiastic about joining forces with displaced Russian scientists. The Academy of Sciences encouraged the United States to fund and hire Russian scientists before third-world dictators tempted them away with well-paying jobs. Other experts were more concerned over the loss to science if Russia's most brilliant minds were not employed.

Dr. Loren Graham, an expert on Russian science and technology at the Massachusetts Institute of Technology, told *The New York Times*, "There are some areas of science where the old Soviet Union was a world leader. There were centers of excellence. If those dry up and disappear, it's a loss not just for Russia and the former Soviet republics but for world civilization."

Many political observers believe that this large group of unhappy troops could form the backbone of a popular backlash against reform. The collapse of morale in an army always raises the danger of a military coup. One frustrated officer warned, "If the state doesn't take care of the army, the army is going to take care of the state."

But the state is busy trying to create a defense structure among the newly formed independent republics. Russia, which did not have its own army, at first wanted a central defense force under a unified command. But with Ukraine wanting to form its own independent army, Russia also announced plans to form its own military.

Challenges of a New World Order

The former Soviet Union was famous for its "five-year plans." From its inception, Communist leaders submitted the USSR to these large-scale, systematic programs that were intended to turn the country into a major industrial and military power. In time, the Marxist-Leninist leaders hoped to convert the entire world to communism. Such deliberate plans to expand a form of government that many considered oppressive turned the USSR into the single greatest threat to the free, or democratic, world.

Today, the Soviet government and its behemoth network of bureaucrats are no more. Ironically, the loose federation of states that has replaced the USSR is eager to adopt the economic and political methods of its former enemies, nations with democratic governments and free-enterprise economies.

The dramatic decline of Communist governments on the international scene prompted many to declare the beginning of a new world order. Indeed, the end of the USSR is in some ways part of a "global revolution." Without the Soviet Union to monitor them, the smaller Communist countries have undergone dramatic political changes of their own. Some have adopted more democratic forms of government. Others—especially the hardline governments of Cuba, North Korea, and Vietnam—have lost their single most important Communist ally.

The United States, which has been building a tremendous defense system since World War II to ward off the "Communist threat," is now re-evaluating the size of its military and nuclear forces. American industries that once supplied the national defense system are now trying to divert their capabilities to non-military products.

The U.S. State department had employed large numbers of Soviet experts and intelligence gatherers to watch our "arch-rival," the USSR. With the end of the Cold War, personnel were asked to apply their detective skills to the fight against drug-trafficking in our own inner cities.

Now that the former members of the secretive and isolationist USSR are anxious to join the economic and political systems of Europe, western industrialized nations face new challenges and responsibilities. The commonwealth requires tremendous amounts of aid to survive the transition from government-owned means of production to private ownership and enterprise. Many nations feel that the free world must do all it can to help the commonwealth become a viable democratic federation. In addition to monetary aid, help for the commonwealth will include reeducating its leaders and its economists to the workings of free-market enterprise.

The new spirit of international cooperation that the commonwealth has made possible has also opened up discussion of some global concerns. Environmental problems, the transition from military to peacetime production, nuclear disarmament, food shortages, and unemployment are issues that concern us all. For the first time, the 290 million people of the huge former Soviet state will join the international effort to protect and improve life on earth.

Revolution from Within

Any moral and financial support from the international community to the republics is welcomed hungrily and appreciated. Helping in the building process of new governments has positive effects for the countries doing the helping: it makes for strong allies later on.

But in the final analysis, it is the people in the new republics themselves who have to do the hard work. They are the ones who have to live with the food and medicine shortages, the lack of things to buy in the department stores, the high prices for basic goods, the frustration with an inefficient system, the feeling of never having enough. They are the ones who have to soldier on, seeing only the smallest improvements in their daily lives, yet continuing to believe that in the long run they will have better lives by working hard and making sacrifices now. After seven decades of communism, the people of the fifteen republics knew they were dissatisfied with the past, and they hope for a better, richer, more satisfying future.

Just as our forbears fought and labored to create a free and independent government that could unite the independent states within it, the people of the former Soviet Union are struggling to create their own democracies. From the ruins of communism, the Commonwealth of Independent States was born. But rather than being strong and healthy at birth, the infant commonwealth is weak and fragile. It is only as strong as the individual republics that comprise it. Internal disputes, fears, and troubled economies have only heightened the tensions that already existed. Some say the commonwealth is not meant to last. Others believe that if the commonwealth is given the care and patience it needs to grow, it will have a chance to survive. As with most things in life and politics, only time will tell.

Chronology

August 1991
Communist hardliners attempt a coup in Moscow to oust Mikhail Gorbachev from power. After three days, the coup fails and Gorbachev is returned briefly to power.

September 1991
Civil war breaks out in the Georgia republic.

December 8, 1991
Leaders of Russia, Byelorussia, and Ukraine meet in the Byelorussian city of Brest to officially declare the end of the USSR.

December 17, 1991
Mikhail Gorbachev and Boris Yeltsin meet in Moscow to discuss an orderly transition of power. They agree the Soviet Union would cease to exist by 1992.

December 21, 1991
Eleven former Soviet republics meet in the Kazakh city of Alma-Ata and sign an agreement to create a commonwealth.

December 23, 1991
Gorbachev and Yeltsin meet again in the Kremlin to discuss the final transfer of power.

December 25, 1991
Gorbachev officially resigns as president of the USSR.

December 31, 1991
The Soviet flag atop the Kremlin is officially replaced by the red, white, and blue flag of pre-revolutionary Russia.

February 1, 1992
U.S. President George Bush meets at Camp David with Boris Yeltsin. Together, the two leaders declare an end to the Cold War and outline new guidelines for future relations between the U.S. and Russia.

February 1992
Uzbekistan, Turkmenistan, Tajikistan, and Kyrgyzstan join together with Iran, Turkey, and Pakistan to form an Islamic common market.

May 1992
The pro-Russia Crimean Parliament votes to declare itself independent from Ukraine in a hastily convened vote.

June 1992
Boris Yeltsin and George Bush meet in Washington for a two-day summit on nuclear arms reductions.

For Further Reading

Fannon, C. *The Soviet Union*. Vero Beach, FL: Rourke, 1990.

Heater, Derek. *The Cold War*. New York: Franklin Watts, 1989.

Kort, Michael. *Mikhail Gorbachev*. New York: Franklin Watts, 1990.

Lye, Keith. *Passport to the Soviet Union*. New York: Franklin Watts, 1990.

Nadel, Laurie. *The Kremlin Coup*. Brookfield, CT: The Millbrook Press, 1992.

Stewart, Gail B. *The Soviet Union*. New York: Crestwood House, 1991.

Index

Acknowledgments and photo credits

Cover: ©Bob Stern/Gamma-Liaison; p. 4: ©Czajkowsky/Associated Press;
pp. 6, 8, 12, 21, 22, 23, 24, 28, 30, 48: Wide World Photos; pp. 9, 45:
©Vlastimir Shone/Gamma-Liaison; p. 11: ©Alain Buu/Gamma-Liaison;
p. 14: Gamma-Liaison; pp. 18, 33: ©Chip Hires/Gamma-Liaison; pp. 27,
32; ©B. Swersey/Gamma-Liaison; p. 29: ©Bob Stern/Gamma-Liaison;
p. 34: ©Nicholas Jallot/Gamma-Liaison; pp. 38, 39: ©Guame Gilson/
Gamma-Liaison; p. 42: ©Reza/Gamma-Liaison; p. 47: ©Porter Gifford/
Gamma-Liaison; p. 50: ©Novosti/Gamma-Liaison; p. 52: Associated Press;
p. 55: ©Brad Markel/Gamma-Liaison.
Maps by Sandra Burr.